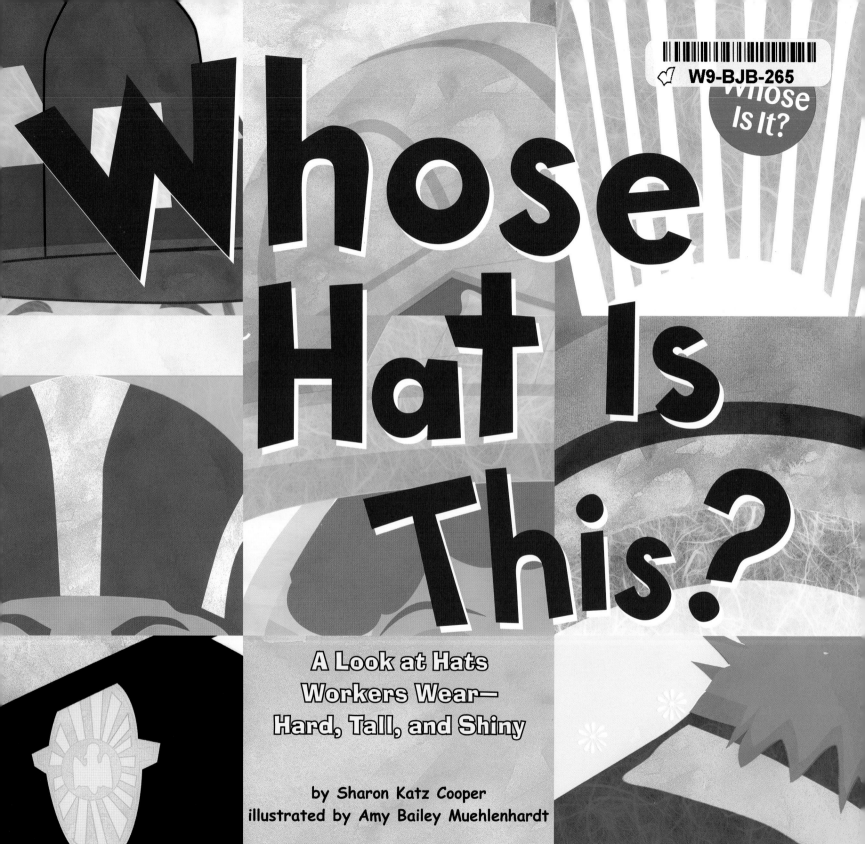

Whose Hat Is This?

Whose Is It?

A Look at Hats Workers Wear— Hard, Tall, and Shiny

by Sharon Katz Cooper
illustrated by Amy Bailey Muehlenhardt

PICTURE WINDOW BOOKS
Minneapolis, Minnesota

Special thanks to our advisers for their expertise:

Rick Levine, Publisher
Made To Measure and Uniform Market News Magazine
Highland Park, Illinois

Susan Kesselring, M.A., Literacy Educator
Rosemount–Apple Valley–Eagan (Minnesota) School District

Editor: Christianne Jones
Designer: Joe Anderson
Page Production: Amy Bailey Muehlenhardt, Zach Trover
Editorial Director: Carol Jones
Creative Director: Keith Griffin
The illustrations in this book were created digitally.

Picture Window Books
1710 Roe Crest Drive
North Mankato, MN 56003
www.capstonepub.com

Library of Congress Cataloging-in-Publication Data
Cooper, Sharon Katz.
Whose hat is this? : a look at hats workers wear—hard, tall, and shiny / by Sharon Katz Cooper ;
illustrated by Amy Bailey Muehlenhardt.
p. cm. — (Whose is it?)
Includes bibliographical references and index.
ISBN 978-1-4048-1600-8 (hardcover)
ISBN 978-1-4048-1976-4 (paperback)
1. Hats—Juvenile literature. I. Muehlenhardt, Amy Bailey, 1974- ill. II. Title. III. Series.

GT2110.C66 2006
391.4'3—dc22   2005021849

Printed in the United States of America in North Mankato, Minnesota.
052016   009789R

Put on your thinking cap and guess whose hat is whose.

There are hard hats and soft hats, square hats and round hats. There are even very tall hats. Some workers wear hats to keep warm. Others wear hats to stay clean. A hat can block sun from a worker's eyes. A hat can protect a head from getting hurt.

Hats come in all shapes and sizes. Can you guess whose hat is whose?

Look in the back for more information about hats.

Whose hat is this, so bright and shiny?

This is a firefighter's helmet.

She runs into burning
buildings to put out fires.
Her helmet keeps her
head safe from falling
objects and extreme heat.

Fun Fact: Firefighters' helmets are red, yellow, or
neon colored so they can be quickly seen from far
away or through smoke.

Whose hat is this, hanging over a face?

This is a beekeeper's hat.

A beekeeper raises bees for honey. She reaches into hives buzzing with bees to get the honey. Her hat covers her face and protects her from stings.

Fun Fact: Beekeepers also wear coveralls and long gloves to protect the rest of their bodies from bee stings.

Whose hat is this, so tall and clean?

This is a chef's hat.

His hat is also called a toque. His white hat shows that his kitchen is clean. The chef in charge of a restaurant wears the tallest hat.

Fun Fact: A chef's hat might have 100 pleats. These pleats show that a great chef can cook an egg 100 different ways.

Whose hat is this, with a polished silver badge?

11

This is a police officer's cap.

It is part of her uniform. A police officer's cap helps people find her quickly in a crowd because no one else will be wearing the same cap.

Fun Fact: The badges, emblems, and nameplate on the uniform are part of the insignia that a person in uniform wears. It shows what town the officer works in or what kind of skills she has.

Whose hat is this, so round and strong?

13

This is a football player's helmet.

When one football player tackles another one, his helmet keeps his head safe if he hits the ground or another player.

Fun Fact: Some football helmets have linings made of inflatable pads. These pads help the helmet fit snugly to each player's head.

14

Whose hat is this, shining in the night?

This is an astronaut's helmet.

It is part of his spacesuit. Up in space there is no air. His helmet gives him air to breathe and keeps his body at a steady temperature.

Fun Fact: It is very cold up in space, so astronauts must wear special suits with their helmets. These suits help the astronauts stay warm.

Whose hat is this,
so hard and yellow?

17

This is a construction worker's hard hat.

Sometimes workers drop pieces of wood or sharp nails while they are working. A construction worker wears a hard hat to protect his head.

Fun Fact: The original hard hat was made out of canvas, glue, and black paint. Today, hard hats are made out of plastic. Plastic is stronger and more durable.

18

Whose hat is this,
so warm and snug?

This is your hat!

When it is cold outside, it keeps your head warm. When it snows, it keeps your head dry.

Fun Fact: Hats can be made from yarn, fleece, wool, cotton, or leather. Some winter hats even have flaps to cover your ears.

Just for Fun

Point to the picture of the hat
described in each sentence.

* I have a special netting to protect a worker's face.

beekeeper's hat

* I have a shiny badge and stand out in a crowd.

police officer's cap

* I protect an athlete's head.

football player's helmet

All About Hats

Important Hats

In Egyptian, Roman, and Greek times, hats showed which people were thought of as more important than others. People who wore bigger, taller hats were more important and held a higher rank in the community.

Hat Talk

People have many sayings about hats. Have you ever heard someone say, "Hats off to you?" That means you did a good job. If a person says "keep it under your hat," it means you should keep a secret.

First Hard Hats

The first hard hat zone in the United States was at the Golden Gate Bridge construction site in San Francisco in the early 1900s.

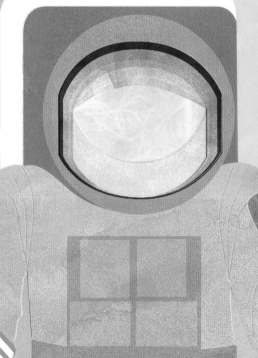

Hat Trick

Three goals made by one player in a soccer game or hockey game is called a hat trick. This started from the British game of cricket in the 1800s. If you scored three times in a cricket game, you were often given a hat by your team.

Glossary

canvas—strong, heavy cloth

construction—to build something

coveralls—a one-piece suit you wear over your other clothes

durable—able to last a long time

inflatable—can be filled with air

insignia—badges and medals that show someone has certain skills or awards

neon—extremely bright

pleat—a special kind of fold

tackle—to knock down another person

To Learn More

More Books to Read

Corbett, Sara. *Hats Off to Hats!* Chicago: Children's Press, 1995.

Morris, Ann. *Hats, Hats, Hats.* New York: Mulberry Books, 1993.

Perl, Lila. *From Top Hats to Baseball Caps, From Bustles to Blue Jeans: Why We Dress the Way We Do.* New York: Clarion Books, 1990.

Whitty, Helen. *Hats, Gloves, and Footwear.* Philadelphia: Chelsea House, 2001.

On the Web

FactHound offers a safe, fun way to find Web sites related to topics in this book. All of the sites on FactHound have been researched by our staff.

1. Visit *www.facthound.com*
2. Type in this special code: 1404816003
3. Click on the FETCH IT button.

Your trusty FactHound will fetch the best sites for you!

Index

Look for all of the books in the Whose Is It? series:

Whose Coat Is This?
1-4048-1598-8

Whose Ears Are These?
1-4048-0004-2

Whose Eyes Are These?
1-4048-0005-0

Whose Feet Are These?
1-4048-0006-9

Whose Food Is This?
1-4048-0607-5

Whose Gloves Are These?
1-4048-1599-6

Whose Hat Is This?
1-4048-1600-3

Whose House Is This?
1-4048-0608-3

Whose Legs Are These?
1-4048-0007-7

Whose Mouth Is This?
1-4048-0008-5

Whose Nose Is This?
1-4048-0009-3

Whose Shadow Is This?
1-4048-0609-1

Whose Shoes Are These?
1-4048-1601-1

Whose Skin Is This?
1-4048-0010-7

Whose Sound Is This?
1-4048-0610-5

Whose Spots Are These?
1-4048-0611-3

Whose Tail Is This?
1-4048-0011-5

Whose Tools Are These?
1-4048-1602-X

Whose Vehicle Is This?
1-4048-1603-8

Whose Work Is This?
1-4048-0612-1

A child's first experience with math can be intimidating. Or it can be as much fun as counting candies! This book assures a positive introduction to early math concepts by combining funny story problems with mouthwatering candy art that will engage the imagination of any young reader.

Read each story with your child and talk to him or her about how to figure out the problem. Discovering the math problem hidden within the words is the key to success with story problems. Have your child try to answer the question by counting the candies on the page. Then turn to the answers in the back of the book and point out how each story problem represents a math problem. With practice, your child will grasp the connections.

It's easy to continue the game in your home and turn your child into a math detective by looking for the math in daily routines. You'll be laying the best possible foundation for building future math skills. See page 32 for some suggestions!

Taffy, caramels, fudgy treats—this book is good enough to eat! If you like candy and you like counting stuff, get ready for a sweet game. Read each of these tasty questions and see if you can figure out the answer by counting the candies in the picture. Sometimes you'll get the answer by counting all the candies. Sometimes you'll get it by counting the candies in smaller groups. The words will give you the clues you need so you'll know what to do. If you get stuck on one, take a guess. It's just for fun—and all the answers are in the back anyway!

You visit the eye doctor on Monday, the ear doctor on Tuesday, and the belly-button doctor on Wednesday. Each doctor gives you 1 lollipop. How many doctor's-office lollipops will you eat this week?

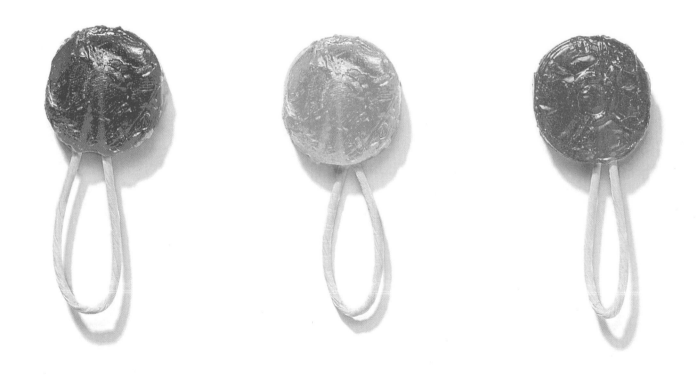

It's Mother's Day! You make your mom a beautiful necklace of gummy rings. You want it to have all her favorite colors. So you use 2 green gummy rings, 2 yellow gummy rings, and 2 red gummy rings. How many gummy rings do you use?

You want to play with your dog, Ruffy. But he's asleep under the kitchen table. You shoot 1 of your gumballs near him. He keeps snoozing. You shoot 8 more gumballs. Ruffy leaps to his paws! He gobbles up all the gumballs you fired at him. How many gumballs does Ruffy eat?

Your grandpa always smells like the butterscotch candies he carries in his pockets. He comes to visit for 7 days. Every day he gives you 1 butterscotch candy. If you save them all up until he leaves, how many butterscotch candies do you have?

You have 4 pieces of taffy. Your best friend also has 4 pieces. But 2 of hers are green. Your best friend hates all green foods! She gives her green pieces to you. How many pieces of taffy do you have now? How many does she have?

Your little brother piles 10 caramels into his toy dump truck. He leaves the truck in the hot summer sun while he watches an ant carry a really big leaf across the driveway. Then he remembers his truck! When he tries to dump the melty caramels, 6 gooey globs are stuck. How many caramels get dumped?

Whack! You hit the piñata at your birthday party. It breaks and 30 peppermints fly out! While you are still blindfolded, the kids at your party grab up 30 peppermints. How many are left for you?

You have 18 jawbreakers. It's bowling day in the pretend world of your dolls. Barb B. needs 1 bright blue ball to go with her bowling shoes. Her friend Kent needs 1 red one. Red is his lucky color. How many jawbreakers are left to suck on?

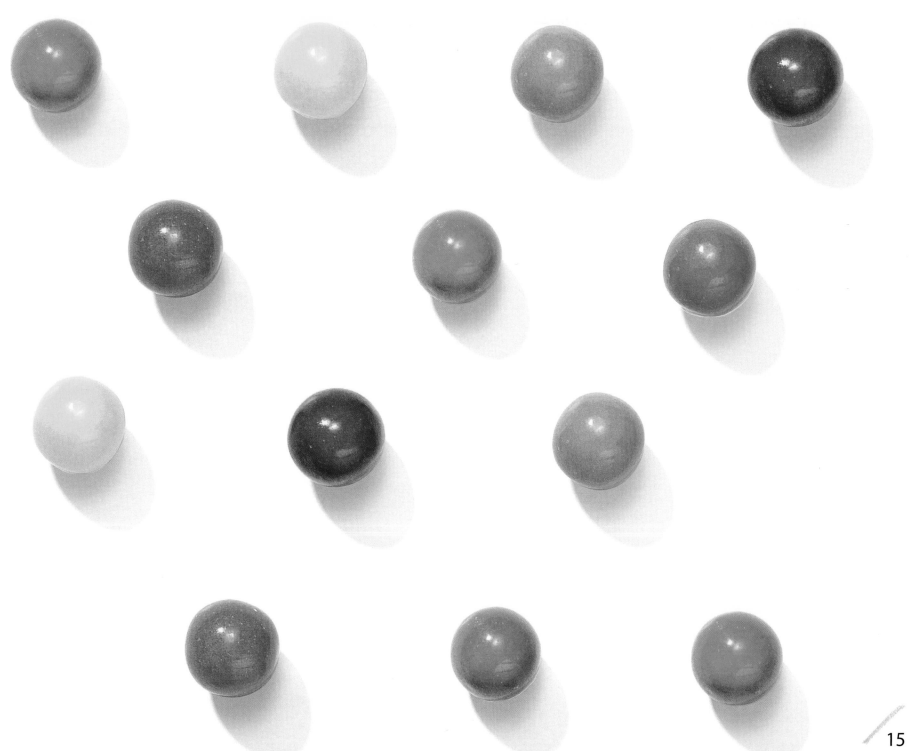

15

It's Valentine's Day! You want to give candy hearts to 28 friends. You need another 1 for your teacher. And, of course, you need 1 for your best valentine, your mom. In all, how many valentine candy hearts do you need?

17

At the scouting cookout, you're the first in line to toast marshmallows. You have a long stick, so you ask for 9. But trying to spear all those marshmallows is hard. Suddenly you feel a big sneeze coming. Splat! Splat! Splat! You drop 3 marshmallows into the mud. How many marshmallows do you have left to toast?

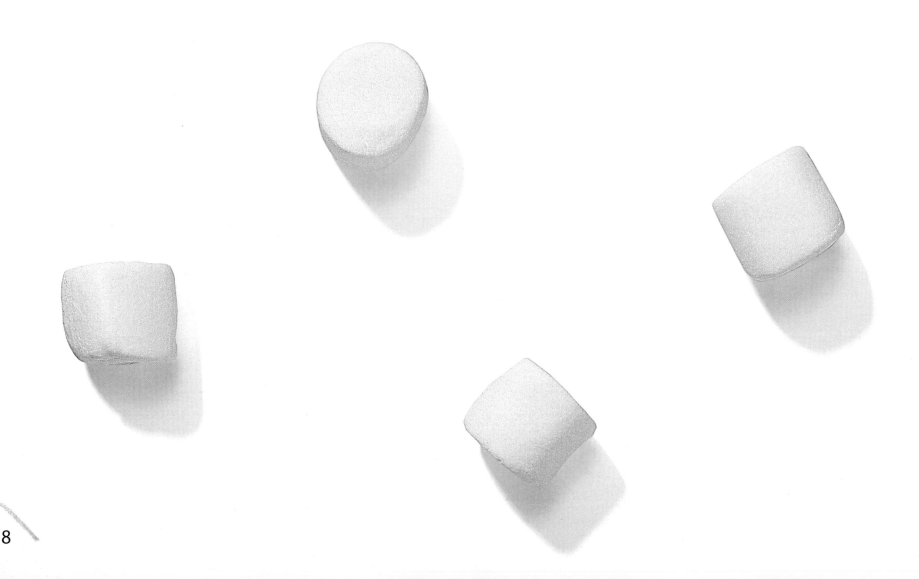

19

The only good thing about visiting your Aunt Beatrice is her dish of red-hots. You politely take only 6 and put them in your pocket. But when she's not looking, you stuff in 20 more. How many red-hots are in your pocket?

On the way home, 10 red-hots fall out of the hole in your pocket. How many do you have now?

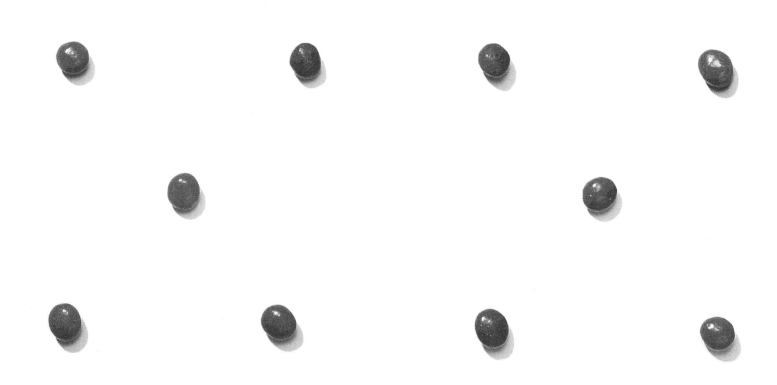

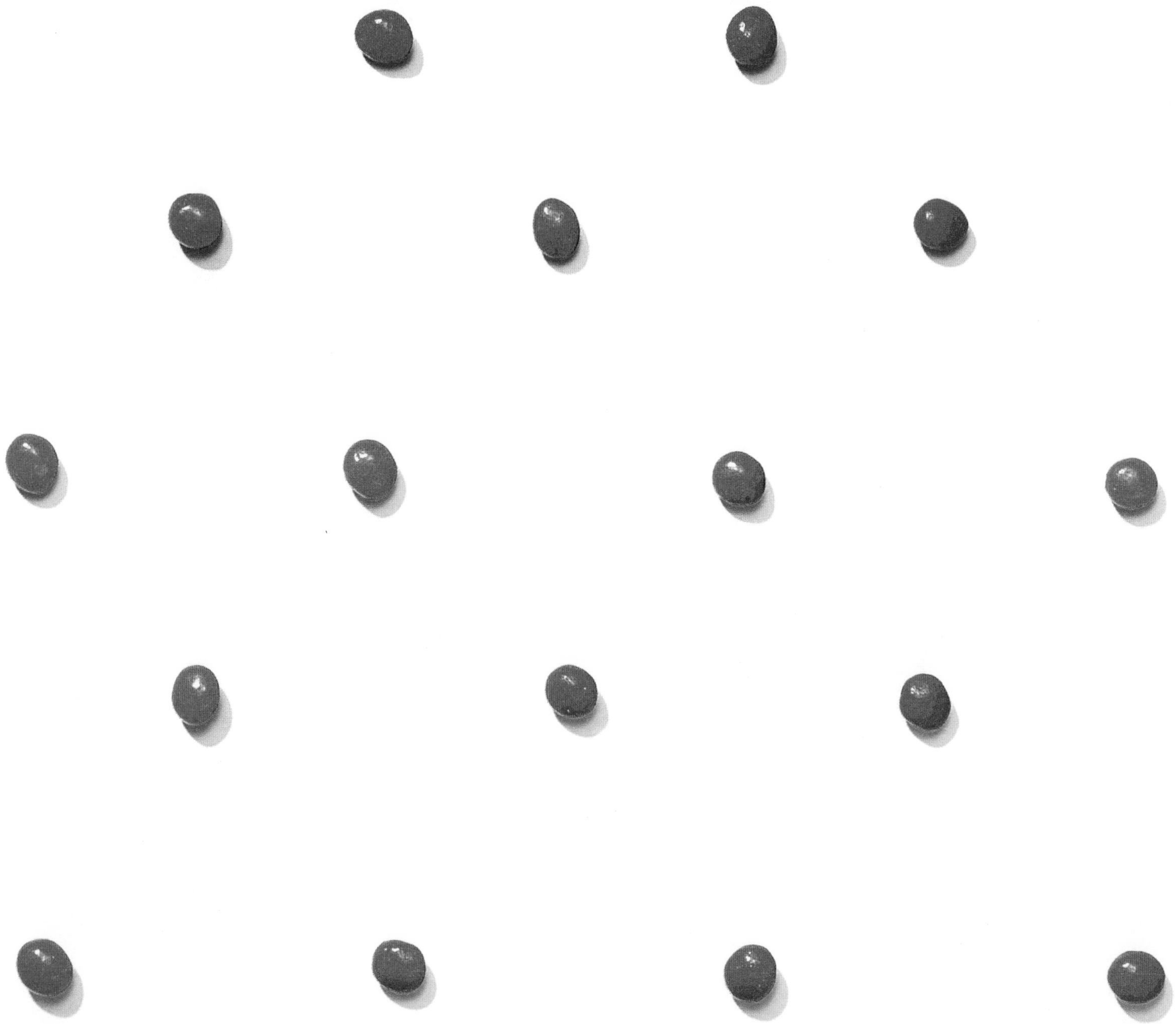

Your grandma makes the best fudge in the world. She cuts it into 20 pieces. You invite your 3 best friends over to share it. But your big sister brings home her 8 best friends to share it, too! If every friend gets 1 piece, how many pieces are left for you and your sister?

It's Halloween, and you have 24 candy corns. Your dad swipes 2 candy corns and sticks them on his teeth like a vampire. He jumps out of the bushes and scares a trick-or-treater, who crashes into you. That trick-or-treater makes you spill 10 candy corns. How many do you have left?

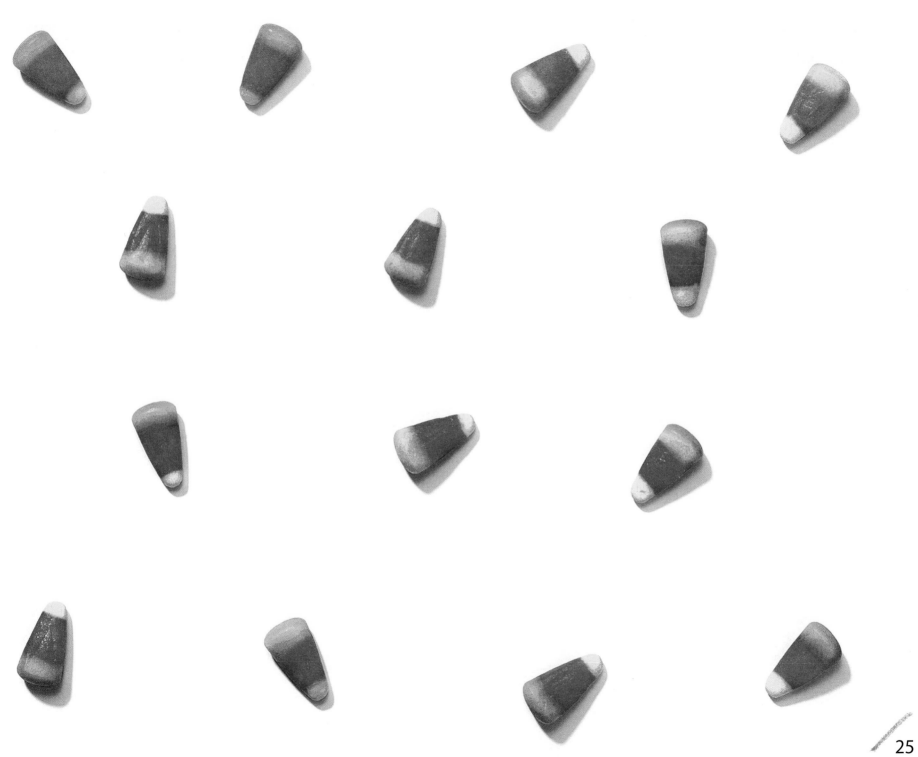

25

It's the 100th day of school! To celebrate, each student in your grade brings 1 piece of candy to school. Ms. Petunia has 33 students in her class. Mr. Rumpus has 32 students. Ms. Dinkle has 35 students. How many pieces of candy does your entire grade have?

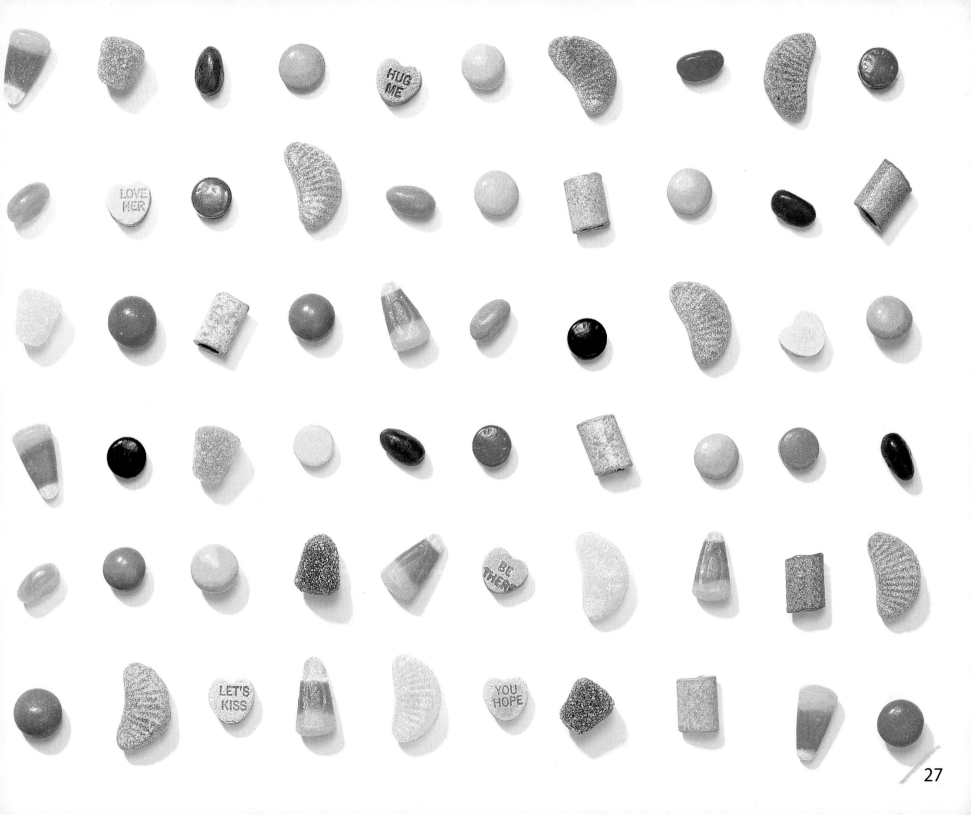

27

Did you like the game? Want to know a secret? It was all math! Look on the next four pages to see how you did. If you were right about how to get the answer but got the wrong answer, don't worry. The most important thing is to figure out how to figure it out! That's math, sweet and simple.

Here's the math!

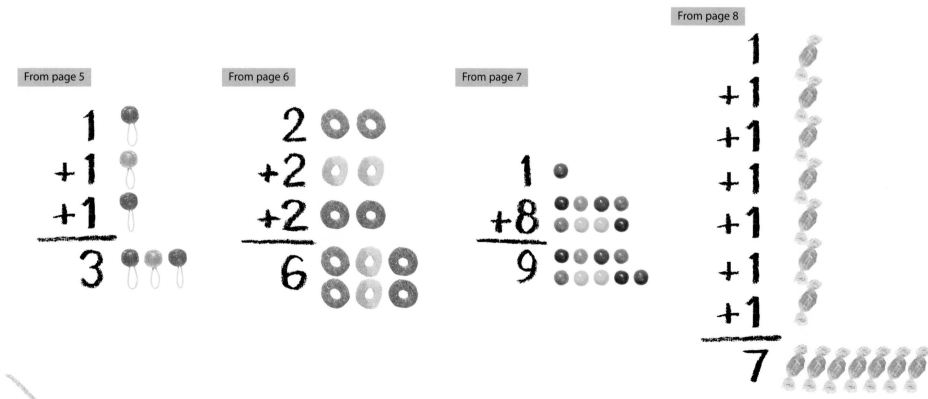

From page 5

$$\begin{array}{r} 1 \\ +1 \\ +1 \\ \hline 3 \end{array}$$

From page 6

$$\begin{array}{r} 2 \\ +2 \\ +2 \\ \hline 6 \end{array}$$

From page 7

$$\begin{array}{r} 1 \\ +8 \\ \hline 9 \end{array}$$

From page 8

$$\begin{array}{r} 1 \\ +1 \\ +1 \\ +1 \\ +1 \\ +1 \\ +1 \\ \hline 7 \end{array}$$

From page 9

$$\begin{array}{r} 4 \\ +2 \\ \hline 6 \end{array}$$

From page 9

$$\begin{array}{r} 4 \\ -2 \\ \hline 2 \end{array}$$

From pages 10 & 11

$$\begin{array}{r} 10 \\ -6 \\ \hline 4 \end{array}$$

From page 12 & 13

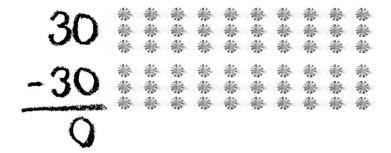

$$\begin{array}{r} 30 \\ -30 \\ \hline 0 \end{array}$$

From pages 14 & 15

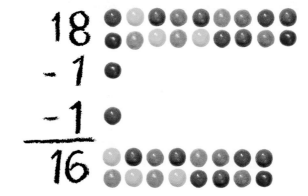

$$\begin{array}{r} 18 \\ -1 \\ -1 \\ \hline 16 \end{array}$$

28
+1
+1
———
30

9
−3
——
6

6
+20
———
26

26
−10
———
16

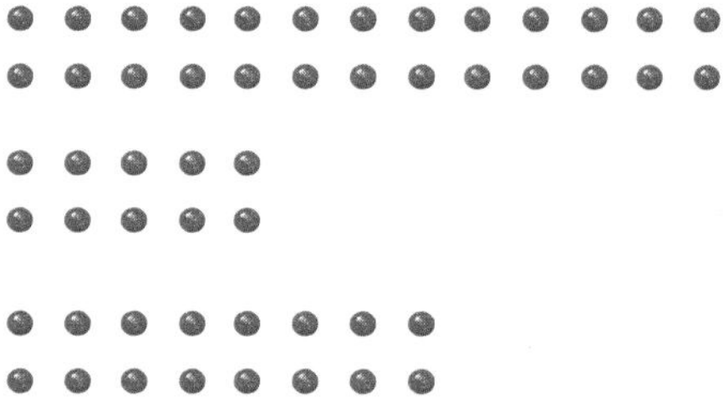

From pages 22 & 23

$$20$$
$$-3$$
$$-8$$
$$\overline{9}$$

From pages 24 & 25

$$24$$
$$-2$$
$$-10$$
$$\overline{12}$$

From pages 26 & 27

$$33$$
$$+32$$
$$+35$$
$$\overline{100}$$

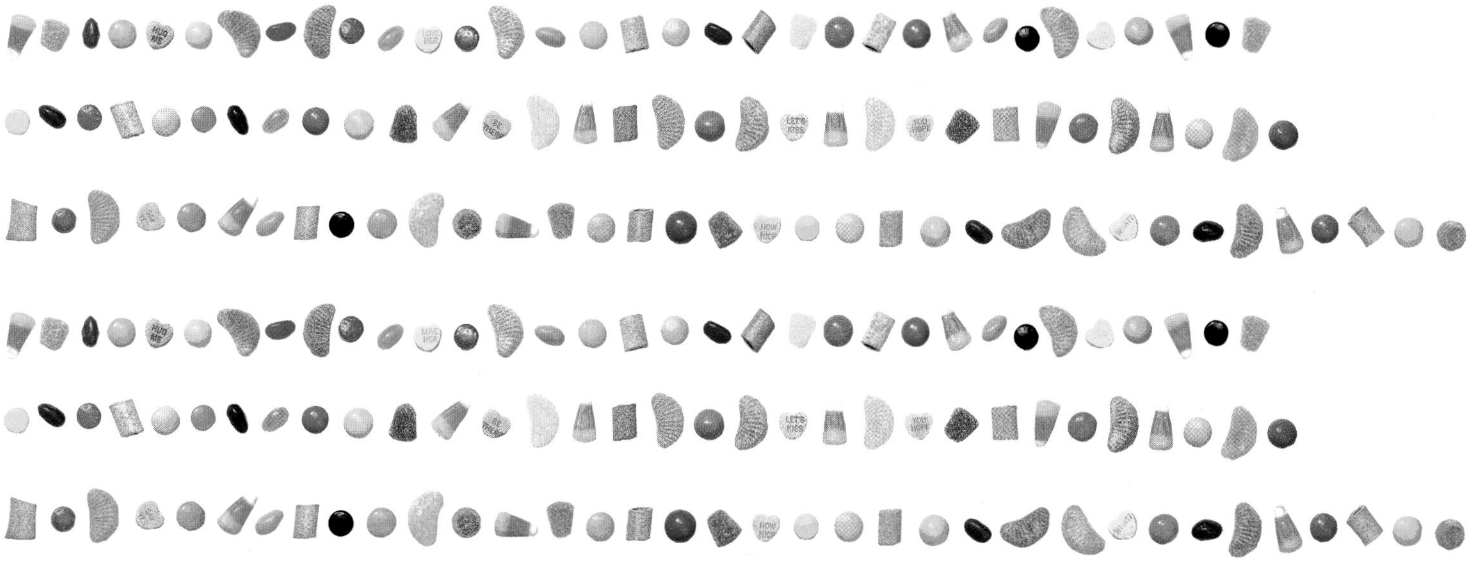

Candy-Counting Activities for Grown-Ups to Do with Kids

• • •

Here are some suggestions for more counting fun in your child's daily life:

● Have your child count how many pieces of popcorn he or she eats during the first Coming Attraction at the movie theater. During the next trailer, let your child count how many pieces you eat. How many did you eat together?

● Bake cookies and let your child count them. When it is time to taste the cookies, ask your child to keep track of how many are eaten, and then ask him or her to figure out how many are left.

● Fill a small jar with jellybeans. Have your child count the jellybeans. Then make a chart. At the top write the quantity of jellybeans in the full jar. Each day, log the number of jellybeans left in the jar. Help your child subtract the number left from the starting number to determine how many were eaten each day.

● Don't limit yourself to candy! Counting fun is all around. Try counting:

  • *the number of legs in your family.* Be sure to include pets' legs! Ask your child to add all the legs together. How many are there?
  • *wheels.* See how many wheels your child can spot in three minutes. Don't forget to add up wheels on bicycles, toy trucks, and in-line skates!
  • *collections.* For example, if you collect teapots and your child collects stuffed animals, have him or her count each collection and add the totals of both collections together.